Editor
Sarah Beatty

Editorial Project Manager
Mara Ellen Guckian

Editor-in-Chief
Sharon Coan, M.S. Ed.

Illustrators
Kevin Barnes
Kelly McMahon

Cover Artist
Brenda DiAntonis

Art Coordinator
Kevin Barnes

Art Director
Cjae Forshay

Imaging
Ralph Olmedo, Jr.
James Edward Grace

Product Manager
Phil Garcia

Publisher
Mary D. Smith, M.S. Ed.

Tracing & Cutting

Author

Susie Alexander

Teacher Created Resources, Inc.
6421 Industry Way
Westminster, CA 92683
www.teachercreated.com.

ISBN: 978-0-7439-3228-8

©2003 Teacher Created Resources, Inc.
Reprinted, 2012

Made in U.S.A.

Table of Contents

Introduction for Parents and Teachers . . 3

How to Use This Book 3

Teaching Fine Motor Skills 4

Tracing

Tracing Ideas 6

Tracing Pages 7

Finger Tracing 7

Street Tracing 11

Tree Tracing 12

Pumpkin Tracing 13

Balloon Matching Tracing 14

Kite Matching Tracing 15

Heart Tracing 16

Job Fill-in Tracing 17

Make-a-Plaid Design 18

Rainstorm Tracing 19

Star Tracing 20

Birthday Cake Tracing 21

Turtle Tracing 22

Spiral Tracing 23

Easter Egg Tracing 24

Cutting

Cutting Ideas 25

Cutting Practice 26

Feather Snipping 29

Make a Snake 30

Pilgrim Hat 31

Star of David 32

Finger Puppets 33

Hearts 34

Bunny Puzzle 35

Quilt Square 36

Shamrock Cutting 37

Cube Cutting 38

Paper Doll 39

Teddy Bear Chain 40

Masquerade Mask 41

Robin and Nest 42

Native American Designs 44

Ocean Puzzle 45

3-D Picture 46

Whole-Class Projects 47

Introduction for Parents and Teachers

What an exciting time of life it is to be 4–7 years old! A child has already learned so much and grown in physical, mental, emotional, and social ways. Now, the young child has graduated to the point of learning real academic skills that will benefit him or her for the rest of life. This series of workbooks will aid the teacher and parent in teaching the child those foundational skills—fine motor coordination, patterning, moving from left to right, cutting, safety skills, and so many more.

This workbook, *Tracing and Cutting*, will focus specifically on those important fine motor skills that many children struggle with and that all children need in order to be successful as they enter school. Skills that seem natural to us as adults need to be learned. These foundational skills are sometimes difficult and frustrating for children at first. In this book, we will teach the skills, learn fine motor coordination activities that will enhance the skills, have practice activities for the skills, and provide worksheets to perfect the skills. You will see a definite progression in the child's skill development as he or she progresses through the activities in the book.

How to Use This Book

This book is divided into two sections: tracing and cutting. At the beginning of each of the sections, the parent or teacher will notice a helpful list of fine motor activities that will aid the child in the skills of tracing and cutting. The activities, then, are listed in a logical progression, with simple, repetitive activities first, followed by more complicated activities, and ending with projects that can be completed with the child's now-advanced skills. It is understood that the child will not work through the activities in this book in a matter of days or weeks, but rather months. Both tracing and cutting are skills that demand much practice.

Remember that tracing and cutting are difficult motor activities to learn. Learning to trace and cut is only possible when a young child is developmentally ready. Please work through some of the small motor activities before attempting the tracing and cutting activities so you can be confident that the child is developmentally ready for this major academic step. Children will find these activities fun and will be willing to try them when they are ready.

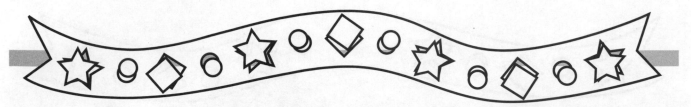

Teaching Fine Motor Skills

Being a child is so much fun! One of the great things about this book is that while the children are learning these extremely important developmental skills, they are having fun! Provide your child with some of the activities listed below to improve his or her coordination and to test readiness for holding scissors and pens.

- **beading**—Use large beads and shoe strings. Progress to finer beads and string, yarn, and eventually thread.

- **button sorting**—Provide a button box with an assortment of colors, styles, and sizes for children to sort as they will.

- **O-shaped cereal**—Have the child move a single o-shaped cereal piece around a cookie sheet or tabletop with his or her index finger; see if he or she can "draw a shape" with the cereal without removing the finger from the piece of cereal.

- **squirt bottles**—Fill some bottles on a warm day and let children squirt each other or the walls and sidewalk with the hand-strengthening activity.

- **finger rhymes**—"Itsy Bitsy Spider" is only one of the hundreds of finger rhymes you can do with the child. There are many excellent books with darling illustrations that you will find at any library or children's section of your favorite bookstore.

Opposite Hand Coordination

Most children have a dominant hand for activities such as writing, eating, and bouncing a ball. Of course, it is important to honor that individuality in a child and not force the body to do something it wasn't intended to do. To discover a child's dominant hand, place a spoon in front of the child at the middle of his or her body. Ask the child to pretend that he or she is going to eat the most delicious ice cream in the world out of a huge pretend ice cream bowl in front of him or her. Say, "Ready, set, go!" and as the child picks up the spoon to eat this delicious dessert, he or she will use the dominant hand.

With that said, though, it is important to develop strength on both sides of the body. So as you work through this book, many of the tracing activities should be done with the dominant and the opposite hand. This should be introduced to children as a game and with lots of laughter, as it will demonstrate interesting results. If the child thinks you are hoping for perfection, frustration and disappointment will be the result.

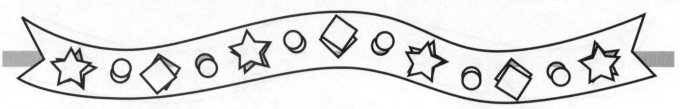

Teaching Fine Motor Skills (cont.)

Teaching Scissor Holding

Teaching a child how to hold the scissors properly can minimize many of the frustrations that revolve around cutting. First of all, show the child how you hold a pair of adult-sized scissors. Next, help the child position his or her hand on a pair of child-sized scissors. (Remember to use left-handed scissors for children with left-hand dominance.) Demonstrate that the thumb always stays 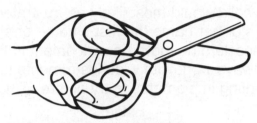 on top while you are cutting. The thumb goes in the smaller of the two holders; two or three fingers go in the larger. Help the child move his or her hand so that the scissors separate. Show how the blades make a "V" that looks like a mouth chomping. Have the child pretend to chomp as he or she moves the blades. Sometimes this is all a child is ready for—save the actual cutting for another day. When the child is ready for cutting activities, move on to page 25 of this book for suggested activities.

Teaching Pencil and Crayon Holding

Holding a writing instrument correctly is not easily done or taught. First, demonstrate how you hold a wide crayon or marker. The first three fingers are the most important when writing. Have the child practice by tapping the middle finger against the thumb. Have the child switch back and forth between tapping his or her third finger and thumb to tapping his or her second finger and thumb. Now, while the child has the third finger tapped against the thumb, slide the crayon in to rest above the thumb. The second finger does the guiding. Have the child "write" in the air before you initiate writing on paper. It is essential that the child starts this process with wider instruments until the motor development is more advanced.

For added help, you can purchase pencil guides at stationery and teacher supply stores that fit over pens, pencils, crayons, and colored markers. These triangular shaped plastic holders mold the fingers into the correct writing position (once it has been modeled).

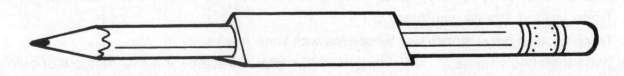

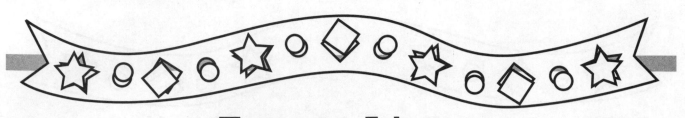

Tracing Ideas

The Progression

A child would most likely be frustrated if he or she were asked to pick up a #2 pencil and write his or her name the first time he or she held a writing instrument. The ability to write requires muscle (fine motor) development in the dominant hand. Until the motor skills are advanced, always work with wide instruments to ease the progression. Following is a suggested list of writing implements to try before using the traditional pencil:

Finger
Large crayon
Wide-tip watercolor marker
Chalk
Thin watercolor marker
Regular crayon
Pencil

Note: Using a ballpoint pen is not advised for early childhood students.

To begin, use the finger for tracing. It is wonderful for motor practice, as well as excellent eye-hand coordination training. Use the index finger as an imaginary crayon. For the child who is not yet ready to put pen to paper, here are some fun and easy activities to try:

- Trace the grout lines in the kitchen tile, pretending that the finger is a car. Always move from left to right.

- Cover the bottom of a cookie sheet with rice, salt, or sand. Trace shapes, lines, and curves in the rice, salt, or sand allowing the pan to show through. This can also be done using a long, flat gift box. Then when the child is done, simply put the lid on until next time. If using a box, glue a brightly colored piece of construction paper to the inside bottom of the box. This will allow the tracings to show up clearly.

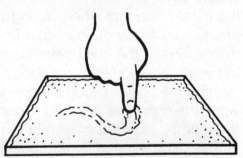

- Cut shapes and symbols out of fine sand paper. Have the child trace over the shapes. Use different fabrics for different tactile experiences. Try felt, furry material, bubble wrap, burlap, or velvet.

- Draw shapes and lines on a whiteboard. Have the child erase them with his or her finger.

Tracing Activities

When the child is ready to move on to more advanced tracing, try some of these activities:

- Trace around a plate with a crayon.
- Trace around large stencils or templates with wide markers.
- Write the child's name in pencil and have him or her trace over it in a rainbow of colors (once in yellow, next in red, then in blue, etc.). The result is a Rainbow Name!

Name _____

Top to Bottom

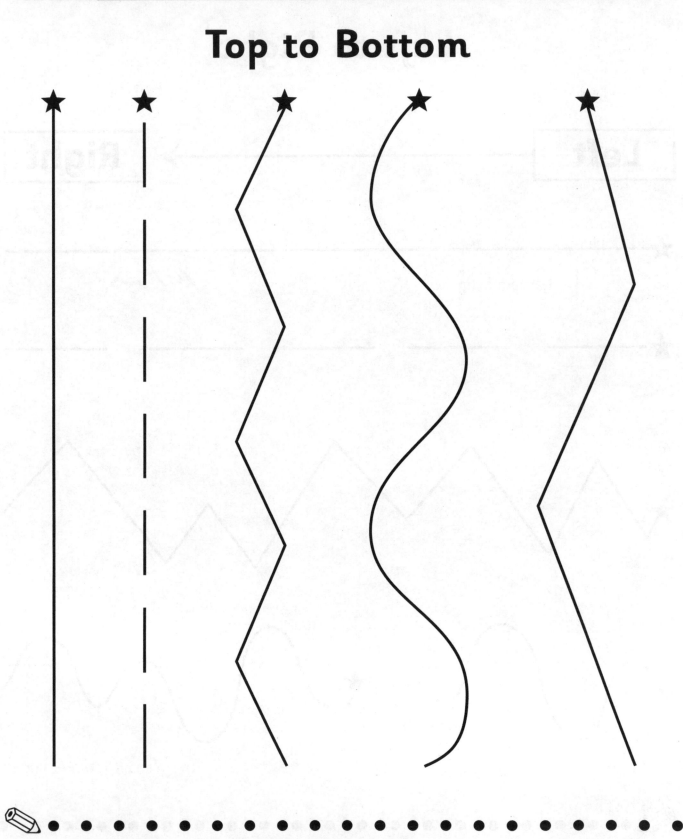

Directions for Finger Tracing: Begin at the stars. Trace these lines from top to bottom. First, use the index finger of the dominant hand, then the opposite hand. Where the line is broken, lift the finger and place it down again on the next line.

Name _____

Left to Right

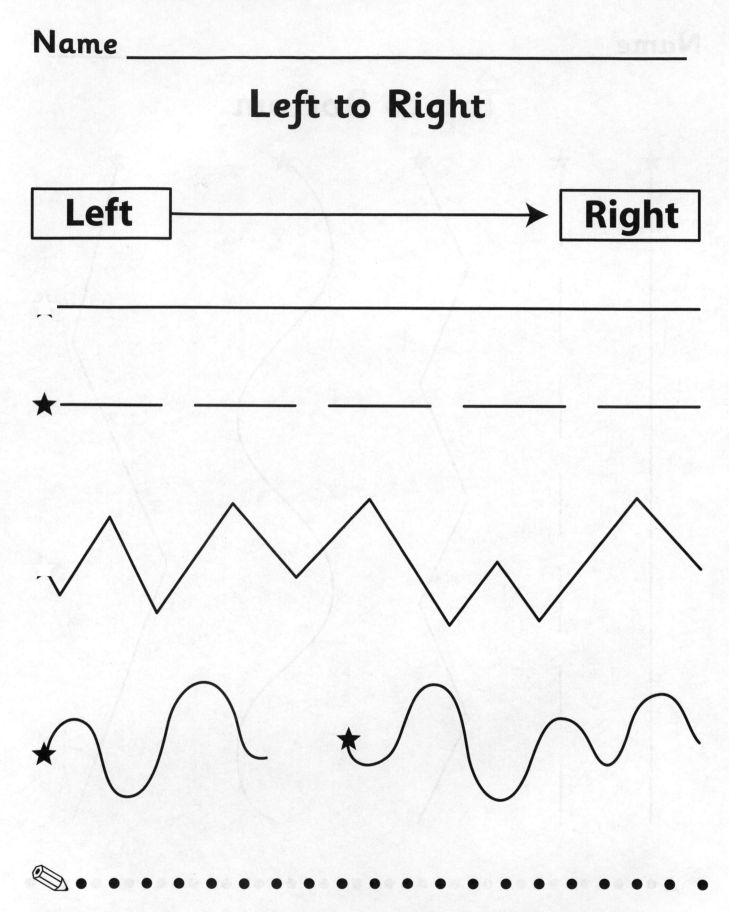

Left ⟶ Right

Directions for Finger Tracing: Begin at the stars. Trace these lines from left to right. First, use the index finger of the dominant hand, then the opposite hand. Where the line is broken, lift the finger and place it down again on the next line.

Name _____

Shapes and Wiggles

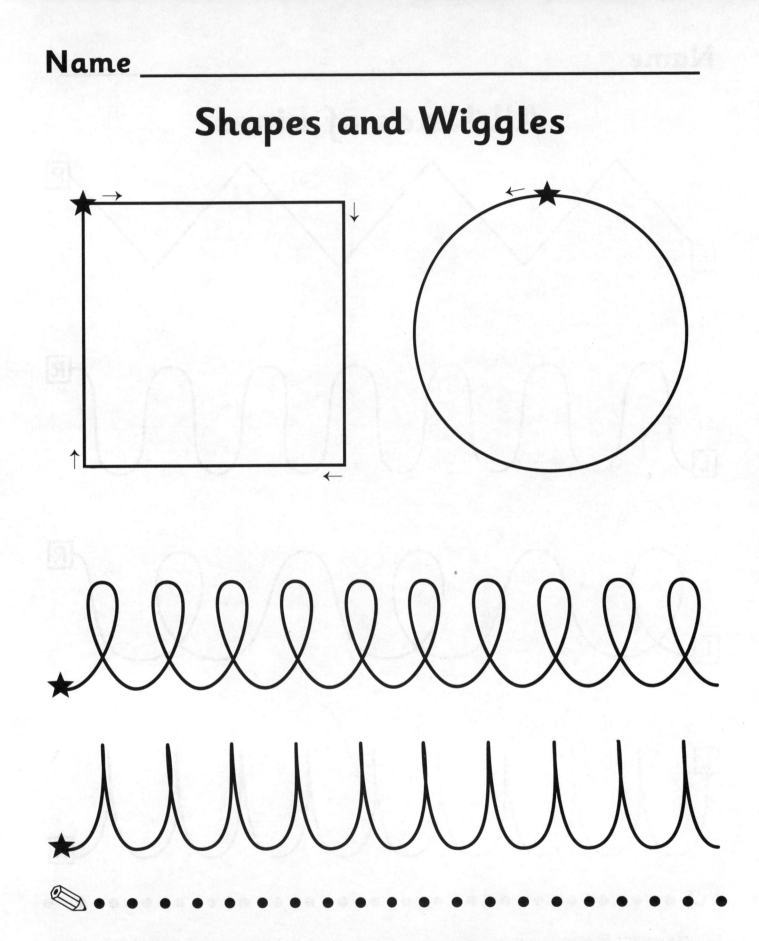

Directions for Finger Tracing: Begin at the stars. Trace these lines from left to right or follow the arrows. First, use the index finger of the dominant hand, then the opposite hand.

9   #3228 Tracing and Cutting

Name _____

All Kinds of Lines

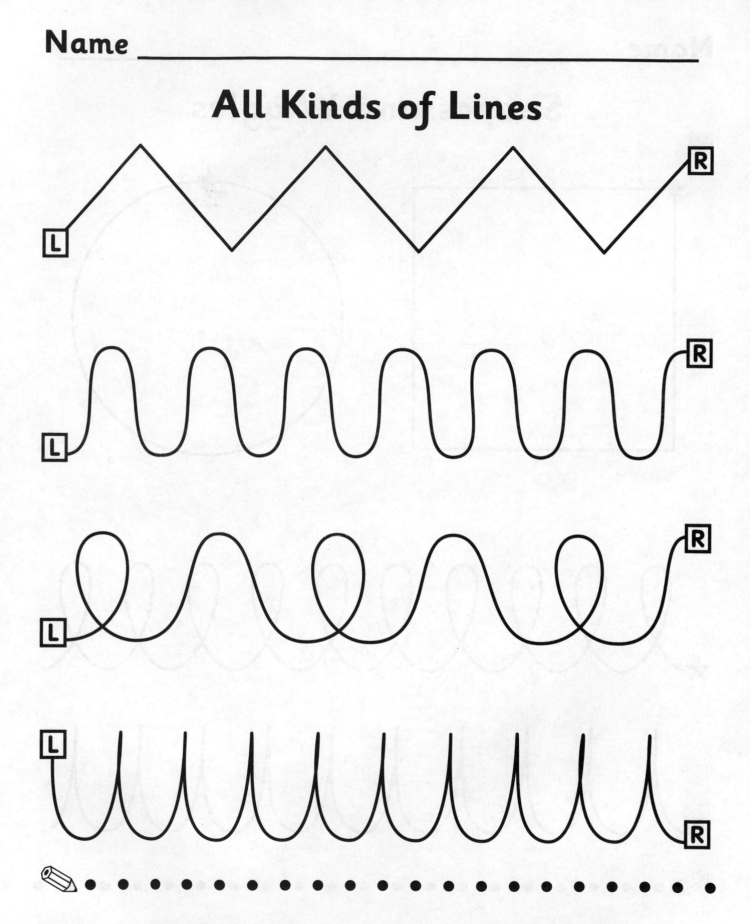

Directions for Finger Tracing: Begin at the "L." Trace these lines from left to right to the "R," using the index finger of the dominant hand, then the opposite hand.

Street Tracing

Directions: Use a small metal car to trace pathways around town. If a car is not available use a block or other small object.

Tree Tracing

Directions: Trace the curved gray lines for the tree lights. Add colored lights to the gray lines if desired.

Name _____

Pumpkin Tracing

Directions: Trace over the gray curved lines in the pumpkins and the curly vines. Color the pumpkins orange with green vines, if desired.

Name _____

Balloon Matching Tracing

Directions: Trace the balloon strings from top to bottom. Color the balloons and the bears, if desired.

Name _____

Kite Matching Tracing

Directions: Trace the kite strings from top to bottom. Color the kites and the children, if desired.

Name _____

Heart Tracing

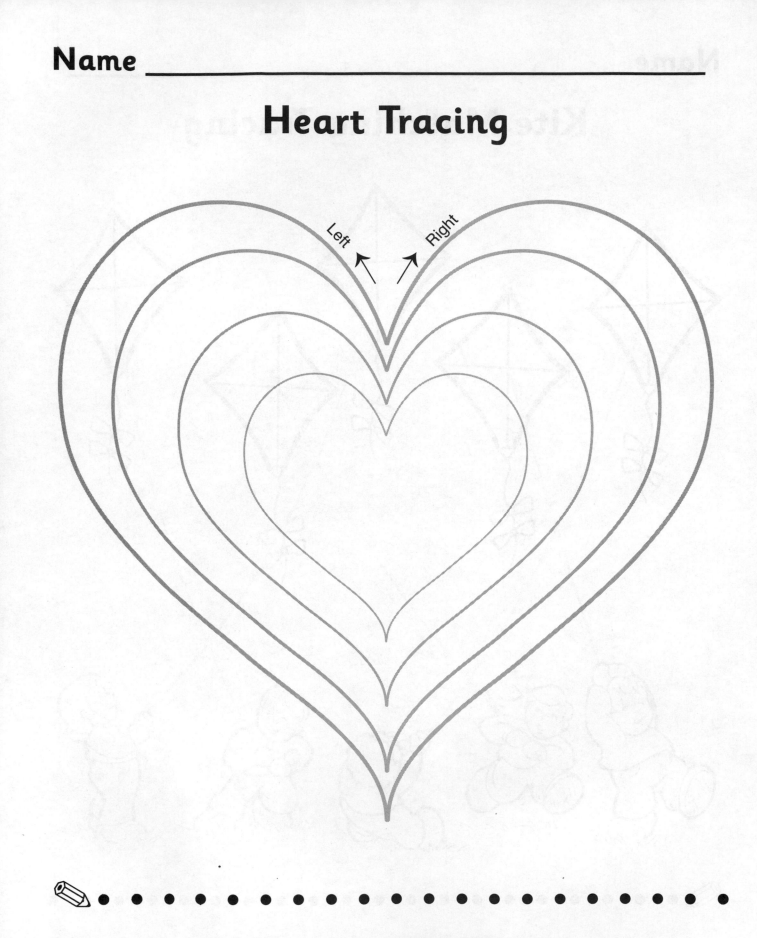

Directions: Trace each heart, from the middle to the right, then from the middle to the left, following the arrows, in various crayon colors. Color, if desired.

Name _____

Job Fill-in Tracing

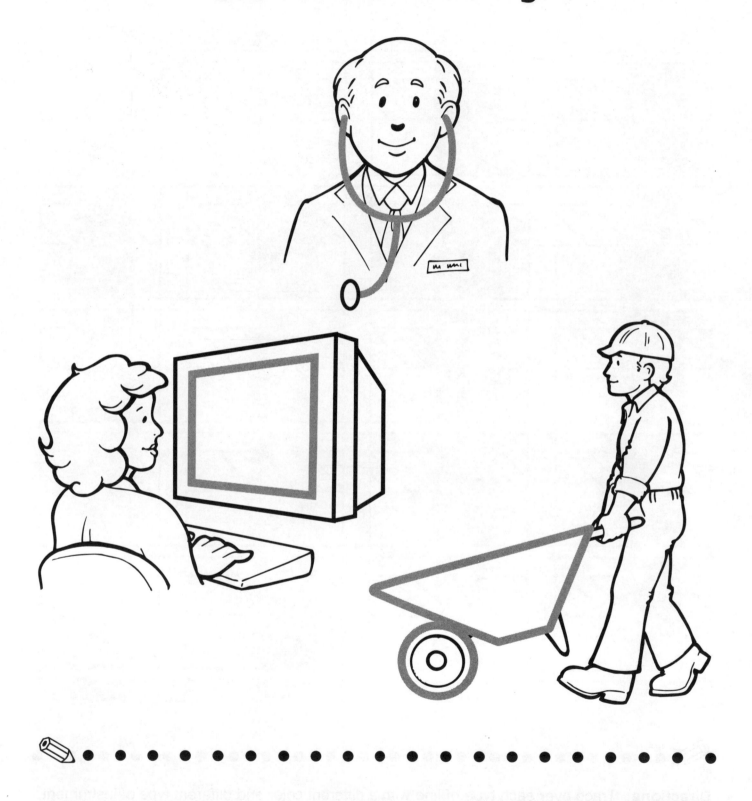

Directions: Finish each person's job equipment by tracing on the gray lines. Color if desired.

Name _____

Make-a-Plaid Design

Directions: Trace over each type of line with a different color and different type of instrument. Choose from wide markers, thin markers, wide crayons, thin crayons, colored pencils, and chalk. Later, laminate this design to make a colorful placemat!

Name _____

Rainstorm Tracing

Directions: Trace the clouds using black or gray. Trace the rain lines, from top to bottom, using blue or gray. Color the clouds.

Name _____

Star Tracing

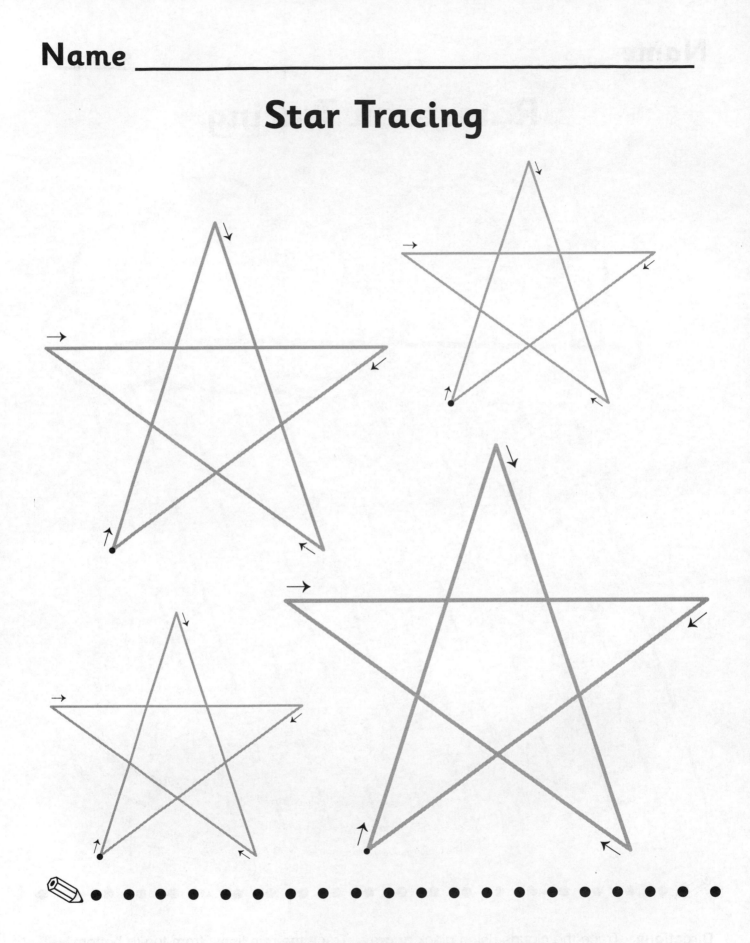

Directions: Start at the dots and follow the arrows to trace the stars.

Name _____

Birthday Cake Tracing

Directions: Trace all of the gray lines on the birthday cake. Color the cake.

Turtle Tracing

Directions: Trace the edges of the turtle's shell and color the turtle and his home.

Name _____

Spiral Tracing

Directions: Start at each dot and follow the arrows to trace spiral designs. Do it in a second and third color to make interesting designs.

Name _____

Easter Egg Tracing

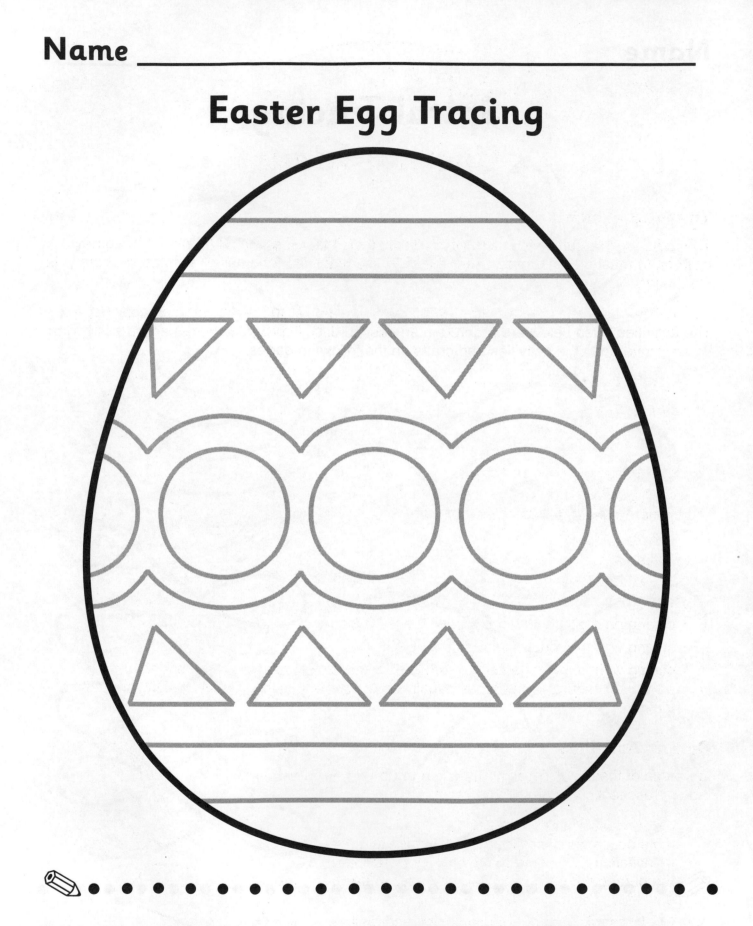

Directions: Trace the shapes and the lines in the egg. Press firmly with the crayon when tracing. Color the egg.

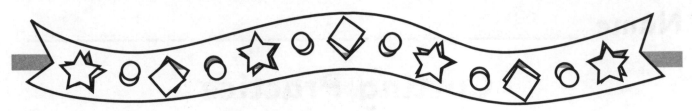

Cutting Ideas

The Progression

The motor skill of cutting is much more difficult than it looks, and it takes longer for some children to master than others. After the child has practiced "chomping" with the scissors, it is time to practice with paper.

For beginners, construction paper or thin tagboard is easier to manipulate than copy paper. The activities listed below are ordered in an easy-to-difficult progression. After practicing with those, move on to the activities and crafts on the following pages.

- tearing (an important precutting skill)
- snipping multiple small cuts, as the child moves the paper
- fringing (using the full length of the scissors)
- cutting straight lines and strips
- cutting sides off one side, then turning the paper to cut off another side
- cutting curved lines
- cutting angles, where a child cuts, stops in the middle of the paper, turns the paper and cuts again
- cutting on a folded edge
- cutting on multiple folded edges or pieces of paper
- cutting with pinking sheers
- cutting with fancy-edged scissors (Note: Fancy scissors are recommended only for advanced cutters. The blades usually do not come together evenly, making the cutting tricky.)

Cutting Activities

Try some of these cutting activities to warm up those preschool cutting hands:

1. Snip pieces of colored paper for confetti. Use as table decorations for a party, to fill a pinata, to add to invitations, or just to throw on a lucky recipient. Encourage the child to cut larger pieces in half until they are tiny.

2. Cut larger pictures out of magazines and mailers to make collages.

3. Practice cutting shapes in half. Start with adult-cut shapes with no dividing lines. Later, add lines that divide the shape into halves.

Name _____

Cutting Practice

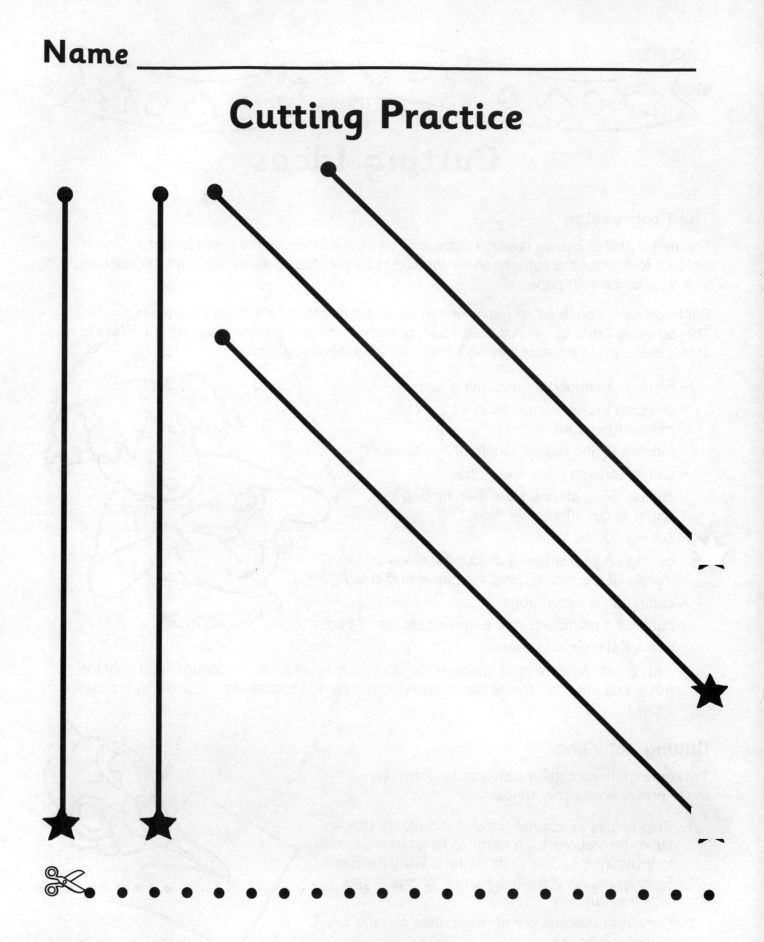

Directions: Begin at the stars. Practice cutting straight lines.

Name _____

Pilgrim Hat

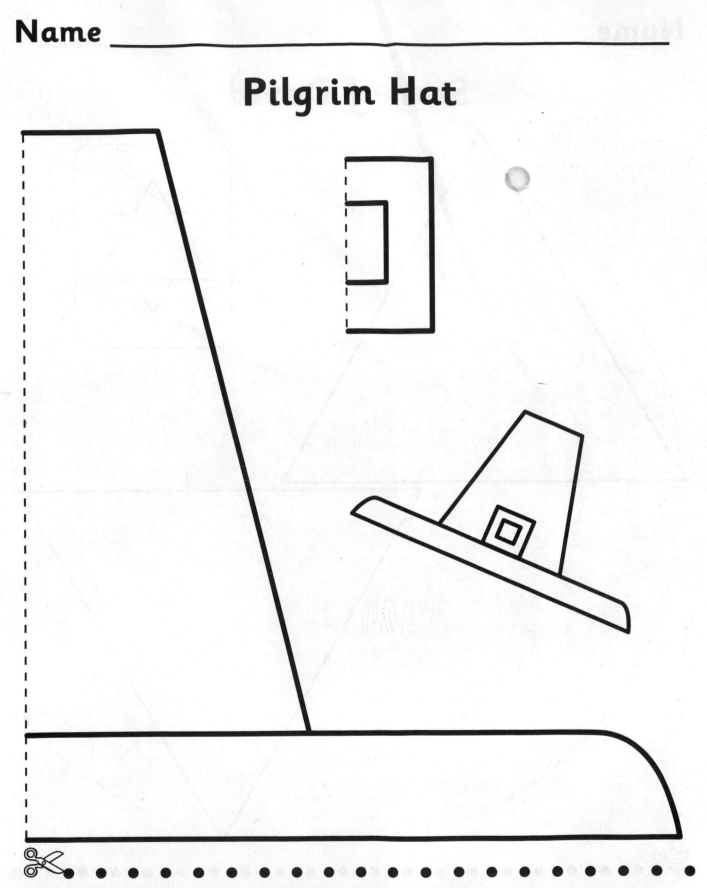

Directions: An adult cuts out the hat pattern. Fold black or brown construction paper. Lay the dotted line of the hat pattern on the fold. Trace and cut out the hat. Trace the buckle pattern onto gray paper. Cut out the buckle pattern. Glue the buckle to the hat. To wear as a hat, have an adult attach hat and buckle to a 2" x 12" (5 cm x 30 cm) strip and staple to fit.

Name _____

Star of David

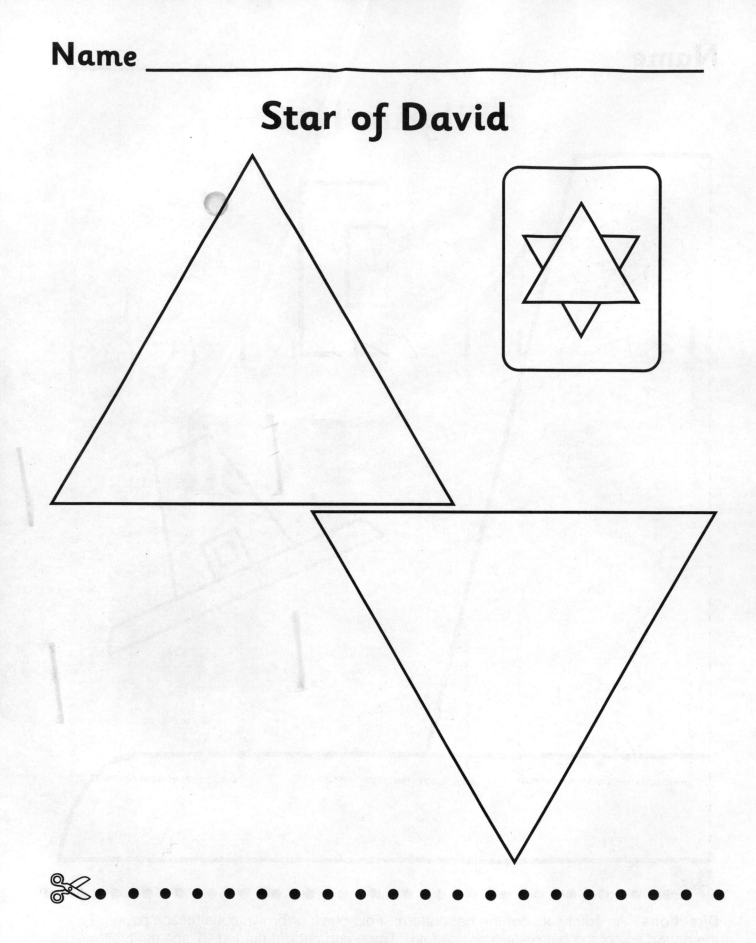

Cut out the two triangles. Glue them together as shown to make a Star of David.

Directions: Cut out the two triangles. Glue them together as shown to make a Star of David.

Name _____

Finger Puppets

girl   boy   teddy bear

girl   boy   teddy bear

Directions: Color the finger puppets. Cut the curved lines around the puppets. Match the backs to the fronts of the 3 puppets. Staple around the edges to complete the puppets. Use the puppets to tell stories.

Hearts

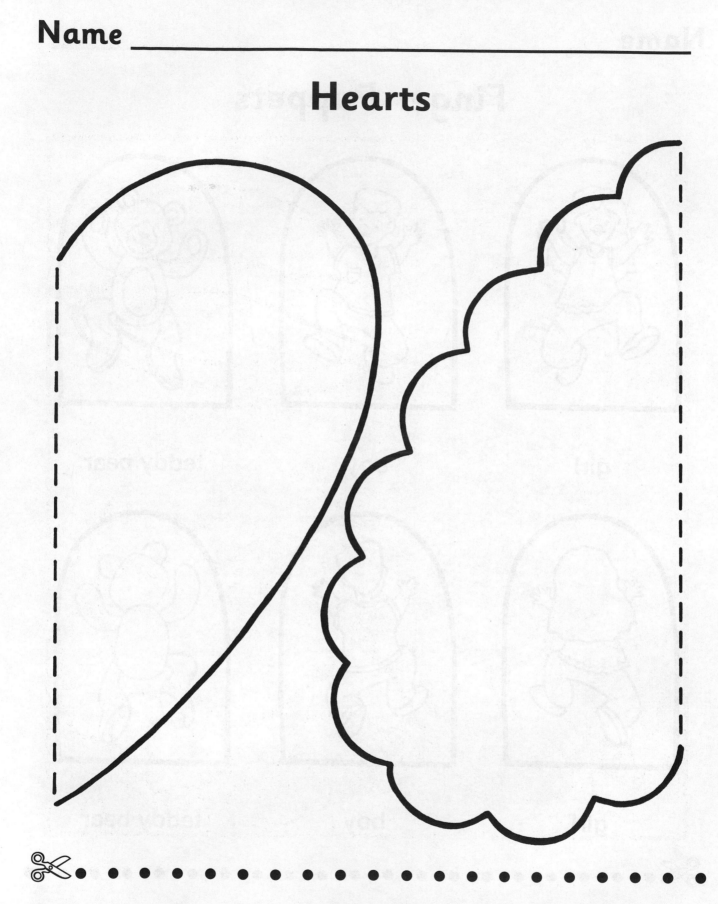

Directions: Cut out the patterns. Fold colored or white construction paper. Place the dashed line on the fold. Trace the patterns onto paper. Cut on traced edges to form hearts. Decorate the hearts with crayons, pens, glitter, etc.

Name _____

Bunny Puzzle

✂ •

Directions: Color the picture. Cut along the dotted lines. Put the pieces back together to form the puzzle.

Name _____

Quilt Square

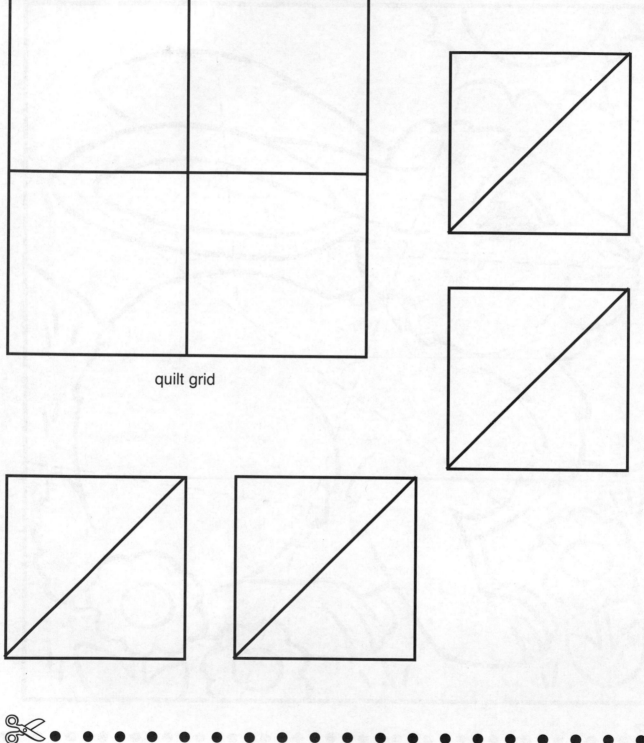

quilt grid

✂ • • • • • • • • • • • • • • • • • •

Directions: Cut out the quilt grid. Color the divided squares with two different colors. Cut out the divided squares and then cut them in half. Arrange the triangles inside the quilt grid to make a design. When the design is finished, glue the pieces to the grid.

Name _____

Shamrock Cutting

Directions: Color the shamrock pieces green. Cut out the pieces. Arrange them and staple the three leaf pieces to the stem.

Cube Cutting

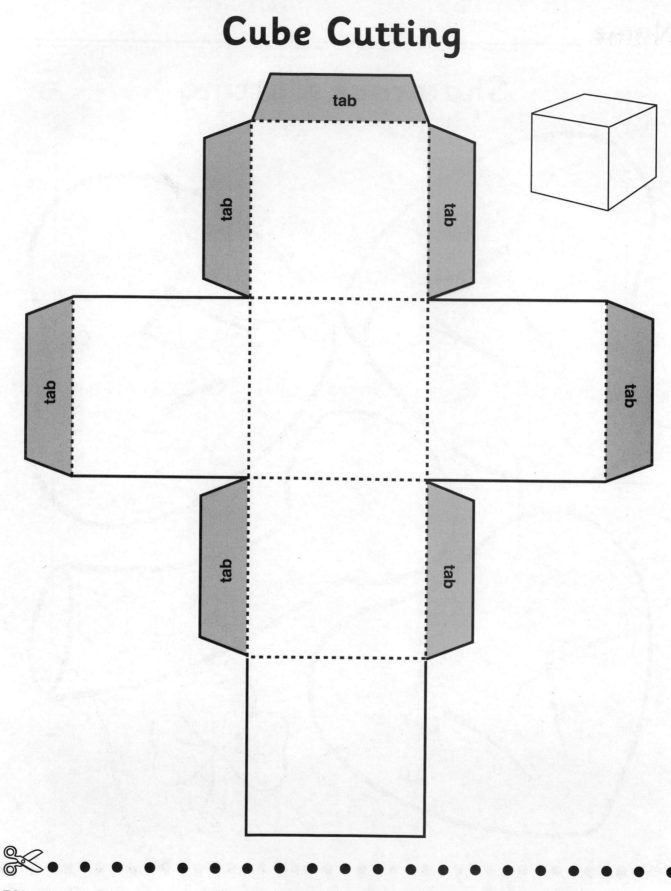

Directions: Cut along the solid lines. Fold along the dotted lines. Glue the tabs to connect the cube pieces.

Optional: Decorate the cube pattern before making it into a cube shape.

Name _____

Paper Doll

Directions: Cut out the patterns. Fold a piece of paper. Place the dotted line of the pattern on the fold of the paper. Trace around the pattern and cut the edges that are not on the fold. Open up the paper and decorate the "person" to look like you!

Name _____

Teddy Bear Chain

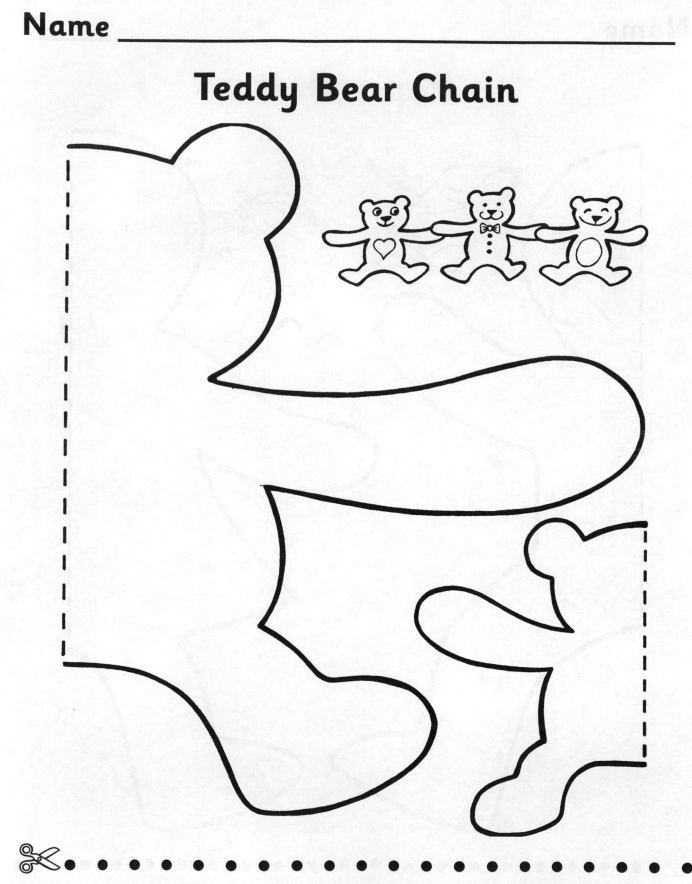

Directions: Trace the patterns onto card stock. Cut out the pattern. Fold the paper so that the edges on both sides match the edges of the pattern. (It might be helpful for an adult to do this.) Trace the pattern onto the folded paper. Cut out the design. Open up the paper to see the design. Decorate the Teddy bears, and tape them together to make multiple bear chains.

Name _____

Ocean Puzzle

✂ •

Directions: Color the picture. Cut along the dotted lines. Put the pieces back together to form the puzzle.

Name _____

3-D Picture

waves

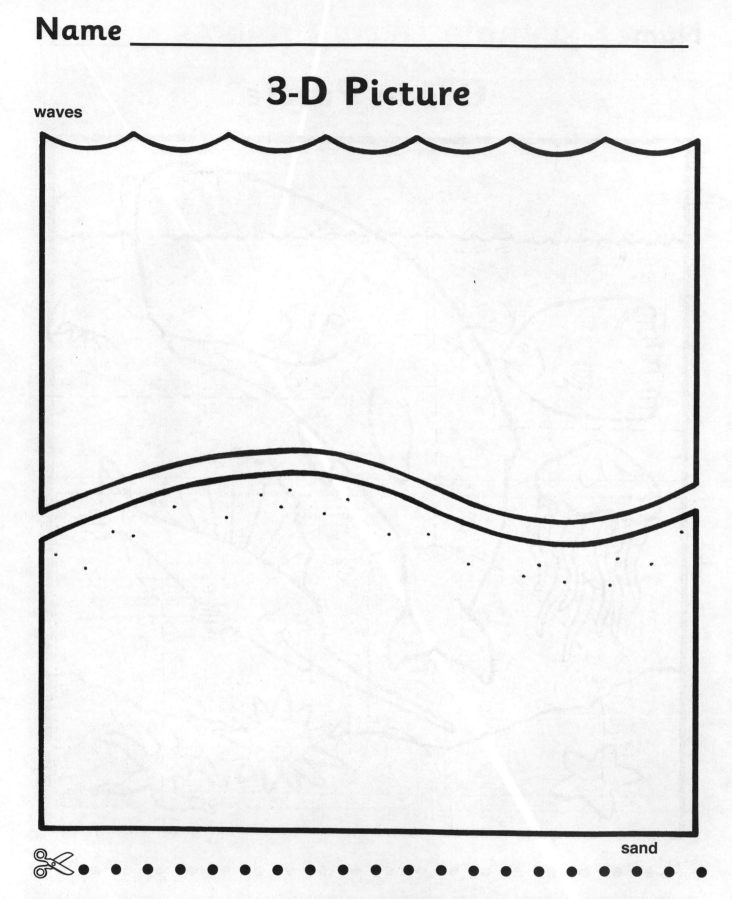

sand

✂ •

Directions: Trace the sand pattern onto fine sand paper. Trace the wave pattern onto foil. Cut out both patterns. Layer them on a piece of light blue construction paper. Add real items, like small shells and fish-shaped crackers, along with stickers of sea animals and birds.

Whole Class Projects

Use your children's advanced tracing and cutting skills to make this mural.

Turkey Mural

Directions: ① Have children trace around each others' spread hands onto white butcher paper. ② Then color the thumb and palm brown and each of the fingers a different color: red, orange, yellow, and purple. Add an eye and a red wattle to the thumb and two stick legs to make the profile of a turkey. Have each child cut around the area of his or her turkey. ③ The children can attach their turkeys to a bulletin board for Thanksgiving. Have them draw a barn, fields, pumpkins, and other fall farm items.

Whole Class Projects (cont.)

Tropical Trees

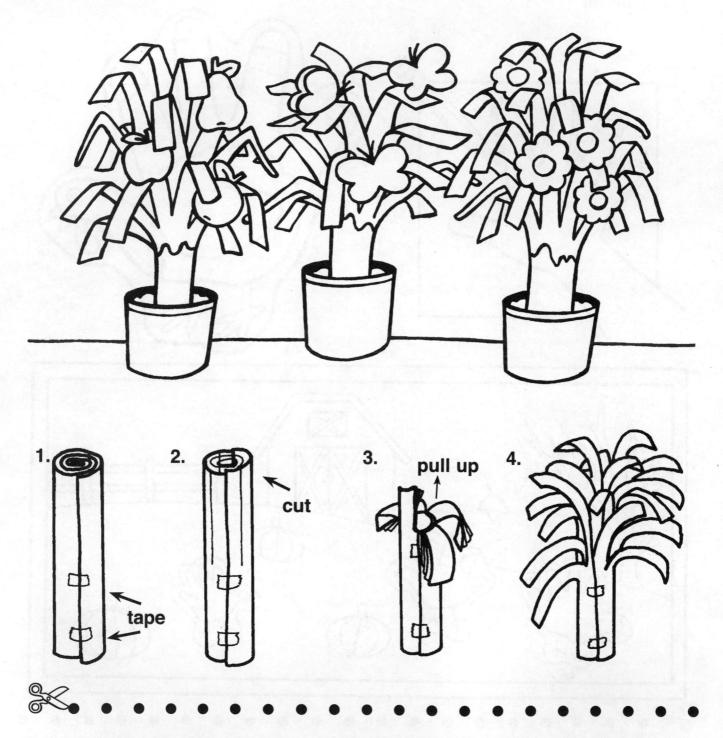

1.

tape

2.

cut

3.

pull up

4.

Directions: Group children into threes or fours. Give each group 6 sheets of newspaper to stack. Starting at the short side, have the students roll the newspaper into a tube about 2" (5 cm) in diameter. Tape the middle and bottom of the tube. Make four 6" (15 cm) cuts into the top of the tube. Reach inside and gently pull the inside strips up and out. Paint the trees and add birds, butterflies, fruit, or flowers. Stand the trees in coffee cans filled with sand or crumpled newspaper.